SALFORD BUS[...]

A fascinating pictorial guide to buses in

by
TED GRAY

Ted Gray

NORTHERN PUBLISHING SERVICE
in conjunction with
MEMORIES

©

ISBN: 1 899181 01 6

Published by   **Memories T/A Castlefield Publications**
Dawson St, Manchester M3 4JZ
in association with
Northern Publishing Services
28 Bedford Road
Firswood, M16 0JA
Tel: 061 862 9399

Written by   **Ted Gray**

Design &
Layout by   *Cliff Hayes*

Printed by   **Manchester Free Press**
Longford Trading Estate
Thomas Street, Stretford
Manchester, M32 0JT
Tel: 061 864 4540

Acknowledgements

The Greater Manchester Passenger Transport Executive kindly allowed access to the records of the former Salford City Transport Department, from which much information was extracted for the author's works on the history of Salford trams and buses. As always, thanks are due to the staff of the Salford Local History Library, to several members of the Greater Manchester Transport Society, and to Cliff Hayes, whose ideas and energy bring works such as this to publication. The illustrations, so important in such a book, are credited individually where the source is known, and apologies are offered for any inadvertent omissions.

Front Cover:- **The author at the wheel of his Salford Daimler Bus. It is leading a procession of preserved vehicles along Water Street (behind the Museum of Science & Industry) in September 1983.**

(photo D. Stubbins)

Back Cover:- **In its after-life as a preserved vehicle, TRJ 112 has made some interesting journeys, none more memorable than when invited to join London Transport's jubilee celebrations at Chiswick Works in July 1983. Before returning home, it was parked overnight amongst the red 'Routemasters' at Stamford Brook Garage.**

(photo Ted Gray)

Additions to the motor bus fleet in the 1920s were mainly single-deck vehicles. Great advances followed the fitting of pneumatic tyres, which made possible a growing number of longer and faster routes. Frederick Road Depot yard in 1929 shows a selection of the motor bus fleet, including two of the ten Dennis top-covered double-deckers, built to a low-bridge design, which enabled them to pass under low railway arches. By this date, the fleet totalled 70 vehicles, 17 older buses having been withdrawn in 1928-29. Also in 1929, a new depot at Weaste was opened to house the growing number of buses, only about one-third of the fleet being garaged at Frederick Road, which was still occupied mainly by tramcars.

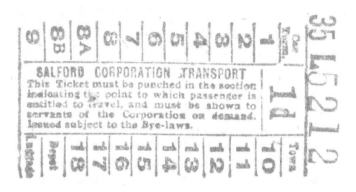

Greengate arches, underneath Exchange Station on the Salford side of the River Irwell, became the rather gloomy 'Manchester' terminus for a number of routes. In March 1931, a Salford bus (one of the 15 A.E.C. Regents with Hall Lewis bodies, BA 7670-84, of 1929), waits to leave on route 3 to Weaste. On the left a double-deck Leyland of the Lancashire United Transport Company (number 30, TF 3567, of 1930) departs on the join route to Warrington. Note that the Salford bus has been adapted to carry tramcar-type stencil route numbers in a roof-mounted box, whilst the L.U.T. vehicle does not display a route number at all. Curiously, Salford buses of 1929-32 used a wooden board, slotted into a metal frame below the canopy, to display destinations. Yet the more versatile roller-blind destination screen was already in use on the tramcars and earlier buses. The boards were reversible, and bore the names of inner and outer destinations on opposite sides. As each board was suitable only for one particular route, their issue, storage, and collection always posed a problem for depot staff.

9

The Crescent, Salford, in 1934, with bus 16 (BA 8942, a 1930 A.E.C. Regent with Hall Lewis body) on service 12 heading towards Manchester, having travelled from Bolton via Little Hulton and Worsley. Note the cobbled road surface with tram tracks, and the early 19th century terraced houses. Off the picture to the right was the meander of the River Irwell as it approached the Adelphi weir.

Radio as you Ride

MARTINS MOTOR TOURS

| FOR REAL COMFORT IN TRAVELLING. | SALFORD. 5. | LET US QUOTE YOU. |

A rival coach proprietor in the 1930s and '40s was J. Martin, also of Cross Lane and also based in a sweet shop only a few doors away from Fieldsend's. Other Salford coach-owners included Hankinson's of Pendleton, Fargher & Wallis of Ellor Street, whose garage was in Frederick Road, and the Pendleton Co-Operative Society, whose garage was in Ellor Street.

Photo S.C.T.

Although buses ordered in the 1920s had been predominantly single-deckers, by the 1930s most routes were operated by double-deck vehicles. However, route 5 (Manchester to Eccles and Peel Green) had to remain a single-deck route because of the low bridge which carries the Bridgewater Canal across Barton Lane. Bus 7 (RJ 7005, a 1937 Leyland Tiger with Massey body) was photographed when new bearing the route 5 details.

The opening of Victoria Bus Station in 1937 did not completely solve the problem of adequate inner termini for the growing number of bus routes. Greengate remained in use. Victoria Bridge Street, having one-way traffic in the Manchester direction from 1933, was also retained as the starting point for Eccles Old Road services. Buses leaving the stands here had to cross the bridge into Manchester, pass in front of the Cathedral, then turn left to cross the river a second time in order to rejoin Salford in Chapel Street. In this 1939 view, bus 174 (RJ 8718) on service 16 to Monton, is halted by a horse-and-cart as it makes the circuit. The approach road to Exchange Station is on the left, and Chetham's School is in the centre distance. Note the increase in road traffic. A Manchester tramcar waits to reverse in the centre of the roadway beyond the bus.

Photo S.C.T.

Not until 1938 did the number of buses exceed the number of tramcars. The year 1939 saw another huge increase in the bus fleet as more tramway routes were converted to motor bus operation. In 1939, Salford purchased only Leyland or A.E.C. chassis, but spread orders for bodies between four manufacturers.

Leyland provided bodies for five of its own chassis, one of which number 230, a Titan TD5) is seen here, photographed in Lancaster Road. This bus (together with number 231) was lent to Coventry in 1941 to ease that town's transport difficulties during the wartime blitz.

Another 1939 acquisition was bus 235 (BBA 560), one of a batch of ten A.E.C. Regents with Park Royal bodies. During the post-war replacement programme, when pre-war vehicles were being withdrawn, this bus was converted in 1948 (along with bus 234) to a dual-control vehicle for driver-training purposes. Consequently, it out-lived its contemporaries long enough to be acquired for preservation and subsequent restoration to its original red-and-cream livery. It now forms part of the collection in the Greater Manchester Museum of Transport.

In the immediate post-war period new vehicles were difficult to acquire as factories returned slowly to peace-time production. The previous General manager had ordered what he could, where he could. Consequently, the 1947-48 period saw Crossleys, A.E.C.s, Leylands, and Daimlers joining the fleet. A new General manager changed the livery from red and cream to green and cream, and the title of the undertaking became Salford City Transport, instead of Salford Corporation. The new manager believed in advertising only Salford City Transport, and so the radiator badges fixed by manufacturers were removed and replaced by others, enamelled in green and cream, bearing the title of the undertaking. One of the 1947 Crossley vehicles is seen here at the Agecroft (Littleton Road) terminus of route 13 in 1954.

Photo Ted Gray

Other 1947 arrivals included 15 A.E.C. Regents, numbers 263-277 (BRJ 917-931). Number 273 is seen here on a Sunday afternoon in April 1958 at the Langley Road terminus of service 34. By this date, the vehicle was used only for part-day services, and , for a time, the 34 was such a route. On Sundays it ran on afternoons only, between Pendleton and Agecroft Cemetery, the short route requiring only one vehicle to maintain its half-hourly frequency. In the background may be noted one of the four cooling towers of Agecroft Power Station, demolished in May 1994.

In 1947 17 Leyland buses (numbered 296-312) ordered by the previous General manager arrived. The new Manager had increased the order by 30 (numbers 313-342), the latter batch, arriving during 1948, bearing evidence of his changed requirements in the shape of larger destination displays. The policy of reserving blocks of registration numbers in advance, made it possible to have the fleet number the same as the registration. Bus 332 (CRJ 332) is seen climbing Rainsough Brow in February 1963, near to the end of its working life in Salford. Service 2 did not normally pass this way, but the usual route via Moor Lane was temporarily closed.

Photo Ted Gray

Photo Ted Gray

C.R.J. 343

WHEN CRJ 343 rumbles down Salford streets the curious wonder how a double-deck Corporation bus taking a load of passengers to work happens to bear the familiar black-and-white "G.B." plaque, which everyone knows signifies that a vehicle has been abroad.

Those with good memories will recall the British Exhibition in Copenhagen just over two years ago, to which one Salford and one Stalybridge bus drove with five other double-deckers from other parts of the country.

Patients in the Royal Manchester Children's Hospital and Hope Hospital benefited by the goodwill trip.

Special fares

Danes liked the English buses so much—especially riding on the top deck—that they paid special fares to travel on top to the German border.

With the fare money the four Salford drivers bought toys for the children.

"We decided to leave the G.B. sign alone," a Salford Transport Department official told me—just as private car-owners continue to flaunt their plaques often years after their trip overseas.

Eight Daimler vehicles, originally ordered for Chester Corporation, were found to be surplus to requirements and were diverted to Salford. Arriving in the autumn of 1948, they were numbered 343-350 (CRJ 343-350). They incorporated the new deep destination display, but had only a single blind for the service numbers, instead of the double blinds, each bearing the 0-9 numerals, on the other new vehicles. Seen at the Duchy Road terminus in 1956, bus 343 retains its GB plate, a reminder of its 1948 visit to the British Exhibition in Copenhagen.

Many pre-war vehicles remained in use pending the delivery of replacement buses. Although the decision to change the livery to green and cream had been taken in late 1946, it was some time before all vehicles were repainted. In this 1948 view of Broad Street, two buses carry the red and maroon wartime livery. Bus 196 (RJ 8740) on the left displays a road safety slogan. This was unusual for Salford, whose Transport Committee resolutely refused to disfigure the vehicles with any form of exterior advertisement. Both vehicles are operating on former tram routes, the old tram tracks remaining buried below the resurfaced road.

SALFORD   CITY   TRANSPORT

(Departmental use only)

Ref. E/JCF/CP	Date 22nd June, 194 8.	
From C.E.	To GENERAL MANAGER.	
Copies to C.A.O. Works Supt. & File.		

SUBJECT Leyland D.D. Vehicle, Fleet No. 44.
Registration No. RJ 6601.

      I would report that the body of this vehicle has now been removed and scrapped, and all seats, glass, electric fittings and serviceable material salvaged for further use as required.

      The chassis will be overhauled in readiness for the fitting of one of the proposed 10 new bodies, this being the fourth chassis for this programme.

Such was the Shortage of vehicles in 1948, that ten of the better chassis of 1934-36 vintage, which would otherwise have been scrapped, were selected to be overhauled, reconditioned and fitted with new bodies, supplied by Burlingham of Blackpool. The ten vehicles were ready in 1949, and were used mainly on part-day peak-hour services. They were allocated new numbers, 101-110. bus 101 (RJ 6602, ex-number 44 of 1936) is seen at the Swinton (Chorley Road) terminus in June 1955, having completed a short-working of service 19 from Cross Lane.

Before 1950 Salford has purchased only 7½ ft. wide vehicles, but, with the approval of the Traffic Commissioners, future orders were mainly for 8 feet-wide buses, allowing a little extra seating space and wider gangway. In 1950-52 a total of 195 Metro-Cammell-bodied Daimler vehicles were purchased, enabling the last of the pre-war fleet to be withdrawn. Bus 426 is seen passing the Fire Station and Cenotaph on the Crescent. The destination display is incorrect, for it is heading away from Duchy Road towards Manchester.

LITTLE HULTON
WALKDEN
BOLTON
LEIGH
BEXLEY SQUARE
WINDSOR PARK
REGENT BRIDGE
CROSS LANE
LANGLEY ROAD
PENDLETON
BURY
IRLAMS O'TH' HEIGHT
DUCHY ROAD
ECCLES CLARENDON CRESCENT

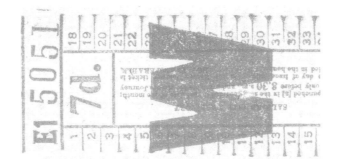

From the local newspaper in 1950.

Nearly replaced

WITH new buses arriving at a steady rate of two or three a week, Salford Transport Department's ambitious five-year plan for the total replacement of its fleet at a cost of over £1M will be completed by March, 1952, I learn to-day.

By then the 210 buses, for which orders were placed in two separate contracts in 1947, will all have been delivered. These, plus a further 92 buses ordered at the end of the war and delivered from 1946-48, will totally replace the fleet that was operating in 1939, when the last purchases were made.

Mr. C. W. Baroth

Second contract

The replacement plan, submitted by Mr. C. W. Baroth a month after he joined the Department as General Manager in August, 1946, was passed by the Transport Committee shortly after, and the first contract for 90 double-decker buses was completed in February this year.

The second contract is well under way. Of the 109 double-decker and 11 single-decker buses ordered, 57 have been delivered within the last three months. The scrapping of nearly 200 obsolete vehicles is proceeding simultaneously.

Mr. Baroth told me to-day: "These are the first buses built to our specifications."

Extra six-inch width—8ft. in all —gives the passenger an inch more sitting space on a double seat and two inches more walking space in the gangway.

Photo Ted Gray

In 1951 services to Swinton and Pendlebury were absorbed into two joint routes, numbered 57 and 77, working across Manchester city centre from Thornley Park and Reddish. Daimler 465 in Station Road, Swinton, is seen arriving via Pendlebury. These routes passed Manchester's trolley-buses along Hyde Road, and at this point connected with trolley-buses of the South Lancashire Transport Company working the circuitous Farnworth to Atherton service. In fact, S.L.T. trolley number 37 is seen on a short-working from Farnworth to Swinton only, but the destination has been turned in advance for the return journey. The date is 21st June 1955.

Photo Ted Gray

The 8-feet-wide Daimlers out-numbered all other types in the fleet, and were to be seen on most routes, particularly the longer ones or those joint with other operators. Service 35 between Manchester and Bury was one such joint route. Daimler 513 is seen in Bury town centre passing Bury 216 (GEN 216, a Leyland PD3 of 1958). Bury's trams finished in 1949, but, as in many other towns, evidence of their former presence remained for years. Here, the tram track has been tarred-over, but can still be detected in the road surface.

THE NORTH-WESTERN TRAFFIC AREA,
ARKWRIGHT HOUSE,
PARSONAGE GARDENS,
DEANSGATE, MANCHESTER, 3.

HOLS

CERTIFICATE No.   **C**   076587

CERTIFICATE OF FITNESS

(Road Traffic Act, 1960)

I, the undersigned, a CERTIFYING OFFICER duly appointed by the Minister of Transport, hereby certify, in accordance with the provisions of the Road Traffic Act, 1960, that the vehicle described below fulfils the prescribed conditions as to fitness in respect

of its use as a......*S.T.A.G.E*.....carriage.

DESCRIPTION OF VEHICLE

Chassis No.....*14639*..   Registration Mark (*See Note below*) | *C R J   418.* |

Make and Model............*DAIMLER   C.V.G.6*.............................

Year of Manufacture of Chassis or first registration..............*1950*....   Seating { Lower deck.....*24*... / Upper deck.......*30*..

Type of Body..............*D.D.H.B*............

This certificate shall continue in force until...*16th APRIL 1970*.........

Date of issue..*18.4.1969*.   ....*Certifying Officer.*

NOTES

1. If the vehicle does not appear to have been registered under the Vehicles (Excise) Act, 1962, that fact will be indicated. In such case the holder of this certificate is required to notify the registration mark of the vehicle to the Traffic Commissioners immediately after it has been assigned and to send or deliver this certificate to them for endorsement accordingly.

2. If any alteration, otherwise than by way of replacement of parts, is made in the structure or fixed equipment of the vehicle to which this certificate relates, the holder of the public service vehicle licence is required to give notice of the alteration to the Traffic Commissioners for the Traffic Area in which the licence was issued.

32

Public service vehicles are subject to regular and rigorous inspection by officials appointed by the Ministry of Transport, and operators are required to maintain the vehicles to a minimum standard of safety. Certificates of Fitness authorise the continued use of the vehicle for a stated period, which may be longer or shorter according to the length of time a vehicle has been in service. This example, issued in April 1969 for a bus which was then 19 years old, was for a period of one year only. That former Salford vehicles were maintained to the highest standards may be judged from the fact that the average life of a bus at that time was 13 years.

In 1955 more cross-city joint services with Manchester were established when two Salford routes from Whitefield were joined with two from East Didsbury and numbered 95 and 96. Two Salford Daimlers, numbers 527 and 476 (with Manchester Leyland 3463 behind), are seen at the east Didsbury (Parrs Wood) terminus.

With the delivery of Daimler 560 (FRJ 560) in March 1952, the post-war replacement programme was complete, and no further vehicles were ordered until 1961. Then 10 Weymann-bodied A.E.C. Reliance single-deck vehicles and 36 double-deck Metro-Cammell bodies Daimlers were ordered in preparation for the withdrawal of the oldest post-war vehicles, which were then nearing 15 years of age. The post-war fleet had been numbered 247-560, with the 1949 re-bodied Leylands being the odd ones out at 101-110. However, the latter had been withdrawn by 1959, and it was decided to begin numbering new vehicles at 101, which was the Transport Committee coach. The front-entrance single-deckers, with under-floor engines, became 102-110. Amongst the first arrivals were 110, parked in front of double-deck 111, outside the old Salford Town Hall in Bexley Square on the occasion of an inspection on the 11th January 1962.

Metropolitan Cammell Weymann Limited Transport Vehicles (Daimler) Ltd. and A.E.C. (Sales) Ltd. request the pleasure of the company of

....

at Dinner on Thursday, 11th January 1962 at the Grand Hotel, Manchester.

R.S.V.P.
General Manager & Engineer,
Salford City Transport.

6.15 for 7 p.m.

The delivery of the first of 46 new vehicles in 1962 was marked by a celebratory dinner, hosted by the body and chassis manufacturers at the Grand Hotel, Manchester. No doubt the hosts were hoping for repeat orders. Body-makers Metro-Cammell-Weymann were not disappointed in 1963-68, but Daimler were to supply only six more vehicles, and A.E.C. none at all.

Thirty of the 1962 Daimlers (111-140) were the last traditional rear-entrance open-platform buses to be purchased by Salford. They were also the last to have the useful rear destination display. New buses were invariably first placed in service on route 15 from Worsley, because the inner terminus was in Manchester's

Piccadilly! TRJ 112 was the last survivor of its class. It was saved from scrap by the author and his family in 1977, and restored to original livery and condition. It is seen after restoration in 1979, outside the Museum of Transport in Boyle Street, Manchester, where it is now one of the vehicles in the permanent collection.

36

Photo the late R.F. Mack

Six of the 1962 Daimlers (141-146) were fitted with what was then (for Salford) a revolutionary design of body, incorporating front-entrances and staircases.

TRJ 141 was photographed at the Warrington terminus of route 10, with Lancashire United Daimler 'Fleetline' 98, also new in 1962, alongside.

37

The first rear-engined full-fronted buses to e bought by Salford arrived in 1962-63. Two Daimlers (147-148) and two Leylands (149-150), both with similar Metro-Cammell bodies, were placed in service, after which orders for the next 55 vehicles reverted to the more traditional front-engined, half-cab style. Leyland 150 is seen leaving Greengate arches on service 3 to Weaste. Regrettably, reasons of economy reduced the attractive three cream bands to only one on these and later new vehicles, and on subsequent re-paints of the existing fleet.

Photo A. Palmer

Victoria Bus Station, viewed from Exchange Station approach road, has Leyland PD2 number 187 of 1963 with two of the 1950-52 Daimlers.

The last half-cab front-engined models were delivered in 1967. Here, 277 (JRJ 277 E) rounds the corner from Bolton Road into Swinton Park Road as the snows were melting in March 1970. At this date, the Salford vehicles had been absorbed into the new South East Lancashire North East Cheshire ('SELNEC', later Greater Manchester Transport) Passenger Transport Executive, formed in 1969, but 277 had not yet received its new fleet number or livery. The buildings on Bolton Road have now all gone in the name of road improvements.

Photo Ted Gray

The last new vehicles to arrive in the Salford livery of green and cream were 20 Park Royal-boded Leyland PDR1s, numbers 304-323, which were delivered in July-August 1969, shortly before the SELNEC take-over on the 1st November. Bus 307 is seen at Monton Green on service 66 from Peel Green in August 1969. Monton Green Railway Station (above the road in the background) had already closed to passenger traffic in May.

Photo Ted Gray

42

The 1969 Passenger Transport Board chose a livery of 'sunglow orange and cream,' but first all existing vehicles were allocated new fleet numbers to avoid duplication. In March 1970 ex-Salford vehicles were renumbered 65-73 (the single-deckers); 3000-3169 (The Leylands), and 4000-4090 (the Daimlers), the latter including 48 of the 1952 vehicles, then over 17 years old. Because of the former combination of fleet and registration numbers, it remained easy to identify Salford vehicles. Here Leyland 215 (now 3061) pulls away from the bus stop outside the Victoria Theatre on Great Clowes Street, Broughton, on the 6th March 1970.

ROAD TRAFFIC ACT, 1960
CERTIFICATE OF OWNERSHIP
BY A
PASSENGER TRANSPORT EXECUTIVE

I hereby certify that the Vehicle of which the Registration Mark and Number are

DBA 215 C

is the property of S.E.L.N.E.C. Passenger Transport Executive

Signed on behalf of the Executive

Secretary.

Date................................

1860w

Ub 0188

EMERGENCY TICKET

1d 2d 3d 4d 5d 6d 7d 8d 9d 10d 11d

Value of ticket shown by punch hole. Issued subject to Regulations. Not Transferable.

SELNEC P.T.E. (CENTRAL) RETURN

1/- 2/- 3/- 4/- 5/- 6/-

PASSENGER

Williamson, Printer, Ashton

Ub 0188

EMERGENCY TICKET

THIS PORTION TO BE RETAINED BY CONDUCTOR AND ATTACHED TO WAYBILL

1/- 2/- 3/- 4/- 5/- 6/-

RETURN SELNEC P.T.E. (CENTRAL)

1d 2d 3d 4d 5d 6d 7d 8d 9d 10d 11d

CONDUCTOR

Williamson, Printer, Ashton

43

Photo Ted Gray

In Salford Ownership, vehicles had been repainted every four years, but in SELNEC/GMT days even as late as 1975 there were still a few green-and-cream examples of the former Salford fleet to be found amongst the sunglow orange. Some were never repainted and retained their old livery until withdrawal. One such was 3008 (ex-157), photographed on 26th March 1975 on Eccles Old Road (corner of Weaste Lane). The

Salford City Transport bus stop had likewise survived. A retrograde step, however, was the replacement of Salford's large, easy-to-read destination blinds by much narrower standardised rolls, with half of the glass aperture being blacked out. In this case, the destination read 'ELLESMERE PK Clarendon Crescent,' in small letters not easy to decipher at a distance. Bus 3008 (157) was withdrawn in 1976 - still green!

44

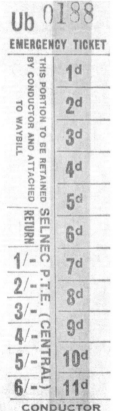

Photo Ted Gray

The redistribution of many former Salford vehicles to other garages allowed them to operate in what had formerly been 'foreign' territory. Here, 3064 (ex-218), now in sunglow orange and cream and allocated to Queens Road Depot, is seen in Albert Square, Manchester, working on the 63 route from Chorlton to Heaton park. Note, again, that half the destination box has been obscured to suit the small letters of the standard GMT blind.

Photo Ted Gray

Two of the ex-Salford open-platform rear-entrance Daimlers (112 and 120 of 1962, renumbered 4001 and 4009) were retained for part-day service long after the others of the batch had been withdrawn. TRJ 120, seen on Eccles Old Road in April 1975, survived until December of that year, and TRJ 112 lasted until February 1977. In its final weeks it was lent first to Princess Road and then Northenden Depots, before returning to join the scrap line at Frederick Road, from where it was purchased by the author.

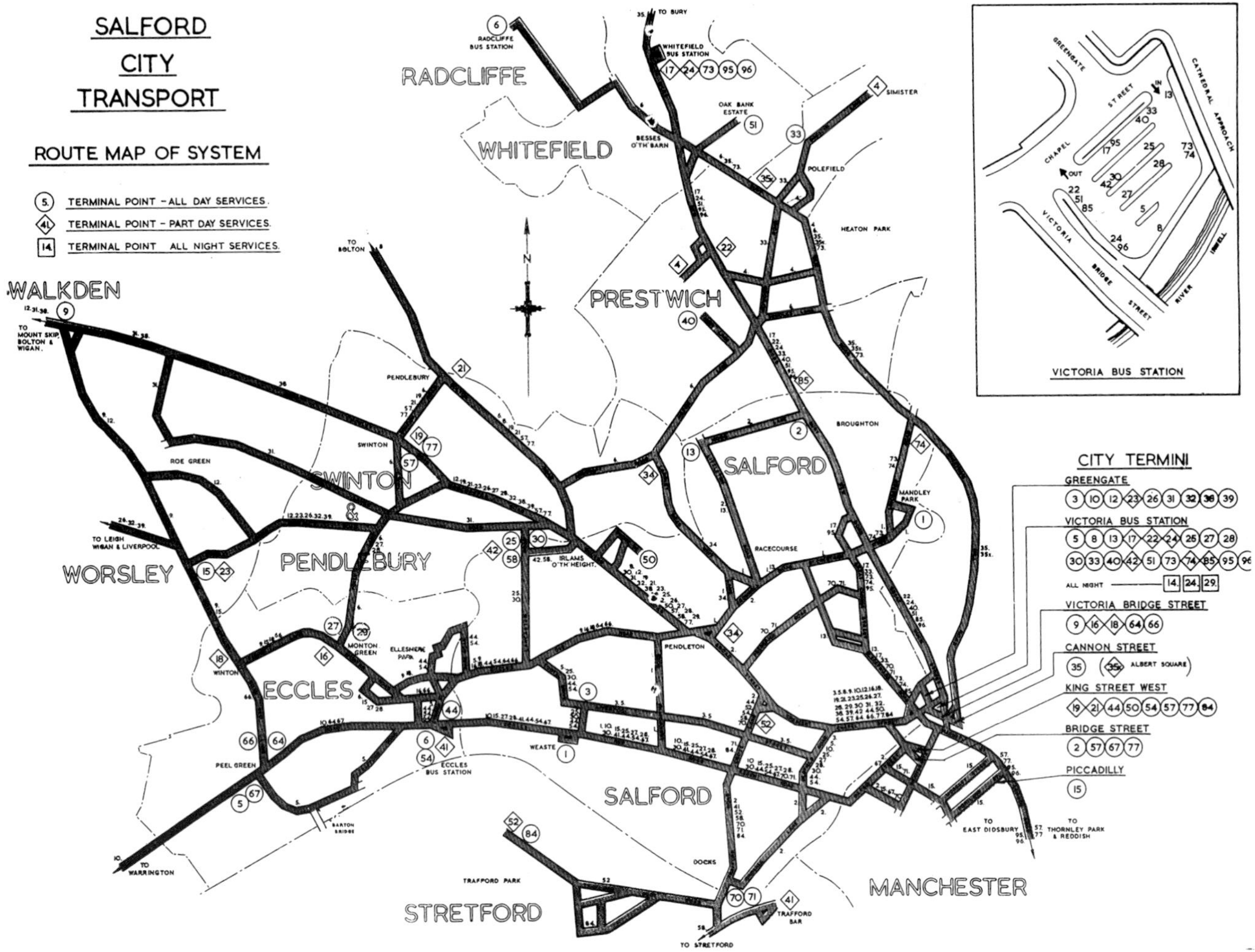
SALFORD
CITY
TRANSPORT
ROUTE MAP OF SYSTEM
5. TERMINAL POINT - ALL DAY SERVICES.
41 TERMINAL POINT - PART DAY SERVICES.
14 TERMINAL POINT ALL NIGHT SERVICES.
RADCLIFFE
WHITEFIELD
PRESTWICH
WALKDEN
SWINTON & PENDLEBURY
WORSLEY
ECCLES
SALFORD
STRETFORD
MANCHESTER
RADCLIFFE BUS STATION
TO BURY
WHITEFIELD BUS STATION
SIMISTER
OAK BANK ESTATE
BESSES O'TH' BARN
POLEFIELD
HEATON PARK
TO BOLTON
TO MOUNT SKIP, BOLTON & WIGAN.
PENDLEBURY
SWINTON
ROE GREEN
BROUGHTON
MANDLEY PARK
RACECOURSE
IRLAMS O'TH' HEIGHT.
TO LEIGH WIGAN & LIVERPOOL
MONTON GREEN
ELLESMERE PARK
WINTON
PENDLETON
WEASTE
PEEL GREEN
ECCLES BUS STATION
BARTON BRIDGE
TO WARRINGTON
TRAFFORD PARK
DOCKS
TRAFFORD BAR
TO STRETFORD
TO EAST DIDSBURY
TO THORNLEY PARK & REDDISH
VICTORIA BUS STATION
GREENGATE
CHAPEL STREET
CATHEDRAL APPROACH
VICTORIA BRIDGE STREET
RIVER IRWELL
IN
OUT
CITY TERMINI
GREENGATE
3 10 12 23 26 31 32 38 39
VICTORIA BUS STATION
5 8 13 17 22 24 25 27 28
30 33 40 42 51 73 74 85 95 96
ALL NIGHT 14 24 29
VICTORIA BRIDGE STREET
9 16 18 64 66
CANNON STREET
35 (35x ALBERT SQUARE)
KING STREET WEST
19 21 44 50 54 57 77 84
BRIDGE STREET
2 57 67 77
PICCADILLY
15